FLAGSHIPS OF MYSTIC SEAPORT

MYSTIC SEAPORT MUSEUM, INC., Mystic, CT 06355-0990

Manufactured in China

Cataloging in Publication data

German, Andrew W., 1950–
    Flagships of Mystic Seaport / [text by Andrew W. German]. —
Mystic, CT : Mystic Seaport, c2000.
      p. : ill. (chiefly col.) ; cm.

    1. Mystic Seaport Museum. 2. Naval museums — Connecticut —
Mystic. 3. Historic ships — Connecticut — Mystic. I. Mystic Seaport
Museum. II. Title.

VM6.U6M9
ISBN: 0-913372-92-7

Flagships of Mystic Seaport is produced by becker&mayer!, Kirkland, Washington
www.beckermayer.com

Text by Andrew W. German
Photographs by the Photography Department at Mystic Seaport.
Historic photographs from Photography Collections, Mystic Seaport.
Line drawings from Ships Plans Collection, Mystic Seaport.

Designed by Rowan Moore for doublemranch
Art direction by Simon Sung
Edited by Marcie DiPietro
Production management by Barbara Galvani

TABLE OF CONTENTS

CHARLES W. MORGAN
WHALING BARK

Launched. . . . . **21 July 1841**
New Bedford, Massachusetts

Length . . . . **105.6 feet**

Length overall. . . . . **133 feet**

Beam . . . . **27.7 feet**

Depth of hold . . . . **17.6 feet**

Tonnage. **313.75**

Although the Charles W. Morgan *does not go to sea, she is often under sail at the wharf as Mystic Seaport staff demonstrate how to set and furl the sails of a square-rigged ship.*

CHARLES W. MORGAN
WHALING BARK

*Born in Philadelphia, Charles W. Morgan
(1796-1861) became one of the leading whaling
merchants of New Bedford, Massachusetts, and
owned the* Charles W. Morgan *from 1841 to 1848.*

Late in 1840, whaling merchant Charles W. Morgan ordered a new whaleship from shipbuilders Jethro and Zachariah Hillman of New Bedford, Massachusetts. Six months later, as much of the town watched, the new ship was launched, and shortly thereafter she was named for her owner.

The American whaling industry was then approaching its peak, with about 700 vessels, and New Bedford was the greatest whaling port in the world. In the 1800s whaling was an essential industry, producing oil for lighting and for lubrication of machinery; spermaceti for candles; and flexible baleen from the mouths of nontoothed whales—called whalebone by whalemen—that was used in ways we would use plastic today.

The *Charles W. Morgan* is typical of the vessels built or adapted for use in the American whaling industry. These vessels had three functions. First, they served as mother ships for six-man whaleboats, carried on davits along the rail, in which the crew chased, harpooned, and killed whales, then towed them back to the ship. Second, they acted as factory ships, with a brick tryworks on deck in which whale blubber was "boiled"–rendered–to extract the oil. Finally, whaleships acted as tankers, carrying home thousands of gallons of whale oil stowed in barrels in the hold.

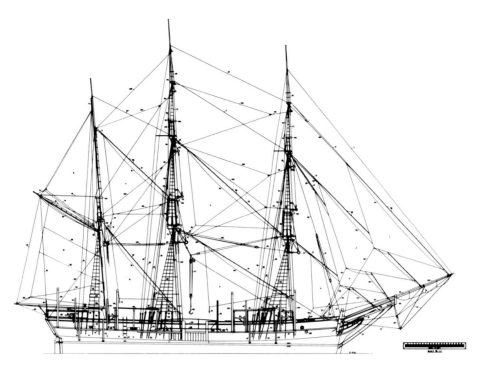

*This rigging plan suggests the complex of lines
used to support and operate both square and
fore-and-aft sails.*

The *Morgan's* service was typical too. On her maiden voyage, which began 6 September 1841, she rounded Cape Horn and cruised the Pacific Ocean. Three years and four months later, having taken 59 whales, she returned to New Bedford laden with 2,400 barrels of oil and 10,000 pounds of baleen worth more than $53,000. During 80 years of whaling she would make 37 voyages, ranging in length from nine months to five years. She cruised the length and breadth of the Pacific, Indian, and South Atlantic Oceans, surviving storms, ice, fire, and even a cannibal attack in the South Pacific. Between 1887 and 1904 she sailed out of San Francisco to be nearer the western Pacific whaling grounds.

During her career, the ship was home to more than 1,000 whalemen of all races and many nationalities. Her crews averaged 33 men per voyage. Like many other whaleships, the *Morgan* sometimes served as home to the captain's family. At least five of her 21 masters brought their wives and even children to sea with them.

Looking aloft on the Charles W. Morgan.

Fast and maneuverable under oars, paddles, or sail, each of the Morgan's *double-ended whaleboats was operated by one of the ship's officers, a harpooner, and four sailors.*

When not engaged in chasing whales, the 30-foot whaleboats were hoisted on davits at the Morgan's *rail.*

As blubber was cut from a dead whale, it was hoisted by a blubber hook attached to the large block and tackle and brought aboard through the opening in the rail. Some of the many lines that operate the Morgan's *sails are belayed on pins at the rail and around the mainmast.*

Small but private, the captain's stateroom includes a gimbaled
(swinging) bed that remains level even when the ship rolls. Captain
Landers installed it in 1863 for the comfort of his wife, the first
of five captains' wives who sailed aboard the ship.

The *Morgan* was originally a full-rigged ship, with square sails on all three masts. In 1867, for the sake of economy, the square sails were removed from her mizzen (after) mast, making her a bark. This rig was typical of New Bedford whalers after the 1850s.

With the development and refinement of petroleum products, plastics, and spring steel, the demand for whale oil and baleen decreased and the American whaling industry declined rapidly, coming to an end in the 1920s. After her whaling days ended in 1921, the *Morgan* was preserved near New Bedford for 15 years as a memorial to the industry that once sustained the region. When support for the ship declined she was turned over to Mystic Seaport and came to the Museum in November 1941.

After 30 years embedded in a sand berth at Mystic Seaport, the *Charles W. Morgan* was refloated in 1973, and has been extensively restored since that time. As she was during her whaling career, the *Morgan* has been mostly rebuilt above the waterline; below the waterline much of the vessel is original. The ship underwent many structural changes during her career. Using the best available evidence, Mystic Seaport's restoration shipyard has restored her to the way she appeared ca. 1905.

The *Charles W. Morgan* is the last survivor of her kind; a veteran of 80 years of hard service in an era of great change. As a museum ship, she is an icon that serves to remind us of the sea's elemental place in American life, of maritime endeavors both brutal and courageous, and of the cooperative human spirit that could forge a shipboard community despite differences in race, background, and language. The *Morgan* is not simply the last American whaler, she is an embodiment of many of the important elements of American social, economic, and technological history. She was designated a National Historic Landmark in 1967.

Becalmed under nearly full sail, the Morgan *has a whaleboat alongside in this 1918 photo. By then she was rigged as a bark, with only fore-and-aft sails on her mizzen (aftermost) mast. Notice the hoops on the fore- and mainmasts where lookouts stood while watching for whales.*

The sailor's view of the Charles W. Morgan, *looking down from the mainmast.*

L.A. DUNTON
FISHING SCHOONER

Launched	**23 March 1921**
	Essex, Massachusetts
Length	**104.3 feet**
Length overall	**123 feet**
Beam	**25 feet**
Depth of hold	**11.6 feet**
Tonnage	**134**

L.A. DUNTON
FISHING SCHOONER

When Captain Felix Hogan needed a new fishing schooner he went to the leading builder of these vessels, Arthur D. Story of Essex, Massachusetts. Hogan wanted a design by Thomas F. McManus, the Boston fish dealer turned naval architect, whose many designs had influenced the form of New England fishing schooners since 1900. The vessel, launched in March 1921 and named for a sailmaker in Boothbay Harbor, Maine, was an up-to-date combination of size, speed, and stability that would serve as home, mother ship, processing plant, and transport vessel for her crew of 20 fishermen.

Ever since explorer John Cabot had returned to England in 1497 and reported the large number of codfish off North America, fishermen had been coming to work the "banks." These shallow places on the continental shelf had all the conditions for marine life, and at the top of the "food web" swam large fish, including cod, haddock, and halibut. Cod were especially desirable because they swarmed across the bottom in large numbers, biting eagerly at baited hooks, and because they were easily dried and preserved with salt. Codfish attracted some of the earliest settlers to the New England coast and remained one of the most valuable products of New England throughout the colonial period.

By 1850, Gloucester, Massachusetts, had become the leading fishing port, and home to hundreds of fishing schooners. These fore-and-aft-rigged vessels, with at least two masts and the larger sail on the after mast, were easier to handle than a square-rigged ship and could sail closer to the wind, speeding the fishermen's return home from the banks.

*With her crew working on their trawl lines around the top of the
after cabin, the* L.A. Dunton *"jogs" under reduced sail on the
fishing banks, ca. 1927.*

On board the L.A. Dunton, Mystic Seaport
*staff often demonstrate how codfish were split and salted for
preservation aboard fishing schooners like the* Dunton.

Like whalemen, New England fishermen traditionally earned a share of the profits of each voyage rather than a wage. They were bound together in a joint venture, where individual skills at fishing or processing fish contributed to everyone's success. The captain led by force of will and the fishermen's trust in his judgment and success at finding fish. The only other officer on board was the cook, who kept the men happy and full of calories for their strenuous work.

About the time of the Civil War, New England fishermen began to fish in a new way. Rather than dangling their handlines from the vessel's rail, they adopted the European trawl line, with many hooks attached at intervals along a line anchored to lie on the bottom. To set and haul their trawl lines, fishermen had to leave their schooners. For this work they chose the strong, stable, stackable dory, originally a flat-bottom beach boat. From the Civil War to the 1920s, schooners carrying dories to set trawl lines caught most of the bottom-dwelling "groundfish" landed in New England. With better transportation on shore, an increasing amount of this fish was landed "fresh," packed in ice rather than salt, further increasing the pace of fishing.

The trawl line was three times as productive as handlines, but the increased work and danger discouraged many from becoming fishermen. Soon "New England" fishermen were immigrants from Northern Europe, from the Portuguese Azores and Cape Verde Islands, from Nova Scotia, or from Newfoundland like the *L.A. Dunton*'s Captain Felix Hogan. For these men, life was better in a New England vessel, even if consumers did not appreciate the hardships and danger that fishermen endured.

For ten years Captain Hogan used the *Dunton* almost constantly. In the winter he usually fished for haddock and cod on Georges Bank and other fishing grounds about 100 miles east of her home port of Boston, spending up to two weeks at a time offshore. After Lent, Hogan would take on heavier fishing gear and lots of bait before heading 1,000 miles east to Newfoundland on six-week voyages in search of large, valuable halibut. At the end of each trip he would deliver his fish to the modern fish pier in Boston, the Atlantic world's second-busiest fish market after 1910, where his fresh catch was auctioned off and transported quickly to markets and restaurants throughout the northeast. If the supply was too large, Hogan might take his catch up the coast to one of the Gloucester companies that still salted cod for markets without refrigeration.

Boston was New England's leading fishing port when the Dunton *was launched in 1921. Her after cabin top served as a work table, with cutting boards for chopping bait.*

Beautiful and functional, fast and seaworthy, New England fishing schooners evolved around 1900 into the form represented by the L.A. Dunton. *Fishermen preferred the fore-and-aft schooner rig for maneuverability.*

When the *L.A. Dunton* was built, Canadian and New England fishermen were competing for supremacy in traditional maritime skills, which were already becoming obsolete. The well-known Nova Scotia schooner *Bluenose* was built to race in these competitions, and Captain Hogan entered the *L.A. Dunton* in 1922, but she was badly beaten by the racing schooners built to challenge the *Bluenose*.

By the mid-1920s fishermen could see that the new otter-trawl fishnet, which was dragged across the bottom by a powered vessel, was twice as productive as the trawl lines set by a schooner with dories. Already Hogan had put a diesel engine in the *Dunton* so he did not have to depend on her sails, but it was clear that the *Dunton* and fishing schooners like her would soon be obsolete. Hogan laid up the *Dunton* in 1931 and sold her in 1934 to a fishing company in Grand Bank, Newfoundland.

Further altered to become a powered vessel with auxiliary sail, the *L.A. Dunton* fished in the old way, catching cod on the Grand Banks, preserving them with salt, and sometimes carrying cargoes of salt cod to market in winter. She made at least one voyage to Portugal with salt cod, returning with a load of salt. Sold again in 1955, the *Dunton* finished her working career as a cargo vessel in Newfoundland.

To represent the important story of New England fishing, Mystic Seaport purchased the *L.A. Dunton* from her Newfoundland owners in 1963. Largely rebuilt and rerigged as she was originally, she is outfitted as a fishing schooner might have been in 1922. She was designated a National Historic Landmark in 1993.

A combined bunkroom, dining room, and living room, the forecastle at the bow was the center of the fishermen's off-duty hours.

Flat-bottom, flaring-sided dories were unstable when light, but when loaded with two fishermen and their gear, and up to a ton of fish, they became seaworthy enough to work safely in the open ocean.

JOSEPH CONRAD
TRAINING SHIP

Launched........................	**11 March 1882**
	Copenhagen, Denmark
Length	**110.5 feet**
Beam	**25.3 feet**
Depth of hold	**13.1 feet**
Tonnage	**217**

JOSEPH CONRAD
ex-Georg Stage
TRAINING SHIP

The iron ship launched into Copenhagen Harbor on 11 March 1882 was an unusual vessel with an unusual purpose. Built by Burmeister & Wain, noted builders of large steamships, she was a small sailing ship with an auxiliary steam engine and the graceful lines of earlier wooden naval vessels. Financed by shipowner and former seaman Carl F. Stage, and named in memory of his son Georg, she was operated by the Stiftelsen Georg Stage Minde (Foundation for Georg Stage's Memory) to train boys planning careers at sea. Schoolships for future merchant marine officers had operated before, but the *Georg Stage* quickly set standards for the type.

With crews of 80 boys aged between 15 and 18, she cruised the Baltic and North Sea while the cadets learned seamanship: fitting out, navigation, shiphandling, steam engine operation, ropework, and teamwork. The six-month tours were rigorous, and not without dangers. Tragically, on the night of 26 June 1905, near Copenhagen, the British steamer *Ancona* rammed the *Stage* amidships, nearly cutting her in two. Sinking rapidly, the *Stage* took 22 boys to their deaths. Raised and rebuilt with four watertight bulkheads, she returned to service in 1906. When it was decided that the 50-year-old ship needed replacement, a slightly larger *Georg Stage* was ordered, and to this day operates exactly as did her predecessor. As for the original *Georg Stage*, after training over 4,000 cadets during 52 years, it appeared that she would be scrapped.

The Joseph Conrad *has been a feature of Mystic Seaport's waterfront since 1947.*

In this time exposure, the Joseph Conrad *glows
against the night sky.*

*Sculptor Bruce Rogers designed a figurehead depicting the author
Joseph Conrad, which was installed in 1934 before
the vessel's round-the-world voyage.*

But along came Alan Villiers, an Australian square-rig sailor seeking a ship for training. Without hesitation, he bought the *Stage* in August 1934. As part of the agreement, he changed her name; as a tribute, and as inspiration for his crew, he christened her *Joseph Conrad* in honor of that master of sea fiction, adding a figurehead sculpted by Bruce Rogers. Gathering a crew of professional seamen, boys, and paying "cadets," he left England to circumnavigate the globe, arriving at New York on New Year's Eve. There, Villiers's dream almost ended, as a gale put the *Conrad* on the rocks.

Repaired, she continued on a two-year journey well described by Villiers in *The Cruise of the Conrad*. Rounding the Cape of Good Hope, the *Conrad* cruised the South Pacific before returning to New York round Cape Horn. On this long trek the little ship proved herself an admirable sea boat.

As Villiers could not afford to keep the *Conrad*, he sold her to G. Huntington Hartford, a wealthy businessman. Reregistered as an American vessel, and outfitted with a diesel engine and other amenities, she served as Hartford's yacht, cruising from her home port of Charleston, South Carolina, and in 1937 racing from Newport, Rhode Island, to Bermuda.

In 1939 Hartford turned the *Joseph Conrad* over to the U.S. Maritime Commission for use as a merchant marine training ship. Berthed at St. Petersburg, Florida, she made training cruises in Florida waters for several years. By 1943 she was used mainly as a floating classroom and berthing ship, and was declared surplus in 1947.

As early as 1938 Mystic Seaport had recognized that the *Joseph Conrad* would be an ideal vessel to fulfill founder Carl Cutler's dream of providing sea training for young people. An Act of Congress was necessary to transfer ownership of the ship, and on 9 July 1947 President Harry S. Truman signed Public Law 167, officially turning the ship over to Mystic Seaport.

Arriving in Mystic on 5 August 1947, the *Joseph Conrad* was renovated for her fourth training career in 1949. Her sailing days long past, she has spent 50 years permanently berthed as an exhibit ship and a base for the Museum's sea education program. Since 1977 the ship has undergone extensive restoration to her hull, deck, and rigging, and now looks much as she did at the time Alan Villiers purchased her in 1934. Although no longer an active ship, the *Conrad* maintains her original purpose in teaching young people the values of experience under sail, even as she demonstrates to the general public the intricate skills of the great age of sail.

As the Danish training vessel Georg Stage, *the little ship sailed the Baltic and North Seas with crews of 80 boys preparing for life as merchant marine officers.*

With a reproduction of a lifeboat hanging from her davits, the Conrad's *120-year-old iron hull reflects the sunset.*

Though stationary, the Conrad *still teaches about
the sea when Mystic Seaport staff demonstrate
how to set and furl a square sail.*

Every line on a sailing ship has its place, and sailors must learn the locations by heart. Identification plates like this were added to help sailors learn when the Conrad *was a U.S. Maritime Commission training vessel.*

In a classic pattern of rope against boat planking, this boat fall on the Conrad *is properly coiled and hung for instant use.*

SABINO
STEAMBOAT

Launched	**7 May 1908**
	East Boothbay, Maine
Length	**45.2 feet**
Length overall	**57.25 feet**
Beam	**15.3 feet**
Actual beam, with sponsons	**: 22.25 feet**
Depth of hold	**5.4 feet**
Tonnage	**24**

Still fired by coal, the steamboat Sabino
*is one of very few active survivors of the
revolutionary age of steam.*

SABINO
ex-Tourist
STEAMBOAT

The age of steam was one of the great transportation revolutions in history, yet it lasted less than 150 years. The Ancient Greeks recognized the potential energy produced when water is converted through boiling into the expansive gas we call steam, but this power was not harnessed until Thomas Newcomen built the first practical steam engine in 1711. A number of inventors put steam engines in vessels, including the American John Fitch in 1787, but it took Robert Fulton and his *North River Steam Boat* of 1807 to prove the commercial value of a steam-powered vessel. Within a few years steamboats were operating along the Atlantic coast and on the Mississippi River, and in 1819 the steamship *Savannah* crossed the Atlantic partially under steam. By the 1850s steam vessels had taken the passenger and high-value trades away from sailing vessels on all but the most distant routes and had greatly increased the pace and reliability of transportation.

 Marine engineers continually improved the efficiency and size of steam vessels, perfecting the screw propeller in the 1840s. From the 1850s to the 1890s they developed the two-cylinder compound and three-cylinder triple-expansion engines to make greater use of the power of expanding steam, and the turn of the century brought the highly efficient turbine engine, turned by a jet of steam. More powerful engines could drive bigger ships. When the 57-foot wooden *Sabino* was built in 1908, 500-foot steel steamships were the standard for traveling across oceans, and large steamboats linked large and small ports all along the coast, on the Great Lakes, and on the nation's river systems.

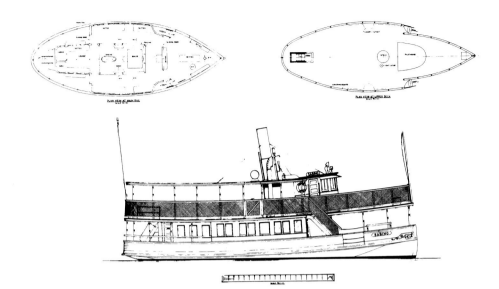

These plans depict the Sabino's *hull arrangement at Mystic Seaport.*

The Sabino's *75-horsepower compound (two-cylinder) Paine steam engine,
similar to this one, has been powering the boat since 1908. (Noank Historical Society)*

As her original name, *Tourist*, implies, this steamboat was intended to provide transportation and mail service between resort communities near the mouth of the Damariscotta River. Launched at the H. Irving Adams shipyard in East Boothbay before the start of the 1908 tourist season, she had little shelter for her passengers, but she had a compound engine, with two cylinders for efficient use of the steam produced in her coal-fired, watertube boiler (in which water passes through tubes in the boiler's firebox, and the resulting steam is collected in the steam drum on top of the boiler before being piped first to the engine's small, high-pressure cylinder, then on to the larger, low-pressure cylinder).

Launched as the Tourist *in 1908, the little steamboat was originally narrower and more open than she is now because she was only used for short summer runs in sheltered waters. In winter she was laid up, as she is in this photo taken at Damariscotta, Maine, ca. 1916.*

The Sabino's *captain uses a bell system to communicate with the engineer. A combination of bells and jingles indicates forward or reverse, and whether to increase or decrease speed.*

After ten years of routine seasonal service on the Damariscotta the *Tourist* sank when the engineer injured himself and the tide swept her under a bridge, drowning the engineer. Rebuilt, the boat was purchased by the Popham Beach Steamboat Company in 1921. The company renamed her *Sabino* after a local hill named for an Abenaki chief. With an enlarged cabin, she ran in summer on the Kennebec River. As in many parts of the country, improvements in roads allowed automobiles and buses to compete with steamboats in this part of Maine by the 1920s. In 1927 Captain Harry Williams bought the *Sabino* to provide passenger service between the islands of Casco Bay, near Portland. Like a seagoing bus, she made the rounds between the islands and the city. In the open waters of Casco Bay, the narrow steamboat was prone to rolling, so Williams added a watertight sponson on either side to widen her beam and make her more stable. A few years later he widened the cabin over the sponsons, resulting in her present arrangement.

The *Sabino* continued to make seasonal runs on Casco Bay until 1955. Long since, the marine diesel engine had been perfected as a cheaper alternative to the steam engine, just as the gasoline-powered automobile had challenged steamboats since the 1920s. After running as a backup boat for a few years, the *Sabino* was retired in 1958 and sold in 1961. The Corbin family of Newburyport, Massachusetts, rescued this last survivor of Maine's coastal steamboats, and they spent the decade rehabilitating her. To tell the story of marine steam power, Mystic Seaport obtained the *Sabino* in 1973. She has been largely rebuilt since then, but her engine is the same one that has powered her since 1908.

Now, in season, visitors to Mystic Seaport may purchase a ticket for a rare steamboat ride, enjoying the quiet power of the *Sabino's* 75-horsepower engine, punctuated by the gong and jingle of the captain's bell signals to the engineer, by the occasional hiss of a steam pressure relief valve, and by the insistent tone of her steam whistle. As small as she is, the steamboat *Sabino* is a very important working example of the motive force that changed history. She was designated a National Historic Landmark in 1992.

Resting on Mystic Seaport's lift dock for maintenance, the Sabino
*shows off her shallow hull and the sponsons that were added on either
side of the hull to make the boat more stable.*

Altered greatly during her 90 years of service,
the jaunty little steamboat Sabino *has looked*
like this since 1967. Today she carries more
passengers than ever during her seasonal trips
along the Mystic Seaport waterfront
and down the Mystic River.